This book
belongs to

. . . .

Oscar, William, Ishbel and Theo – all my love
A.W.

ANNA WRIGHT was born and raised deep in the Scottish countryside of Dumfriesshire, near a tiny village called Tynron. From a farming family, she grew up with animals all around her and, living as she did in the remote countryside, she learned to become creative in her spare time.

Anna studied at Edinburgh College of Art, where initially she wanted to pursue her interest in costume and textiles, but soon fell in love with illustration. Over the years she has built up a business selling her art and designs, operating from both Edinburgh and London. Anna's work has been featured in *House & Garden*, *Country Life*, and *Artists & Illustrators*. This is her second book. You can find Anna at **www.annawright.co.uk** and on Instagram: **@annawrightillustration**

ff

FABER & FABER

MAGNIFICENT CREATURES

Animals on the Move!

The world is full of magnificent creatures great and small, in all their multitude of shades and colours, with their speckled feathers, patterned shells, their unique brand of camouflage. As an artist I am constantly inspired by the extraordinary patterns and detail within nature. I am also intrigued by animal behaviour and character. I use colour, fabric and feathers, my dipping pen and ink in an attempt to express the everyday joy, drama and flamboyance of the animal kingdom. From zebra galloping in their droves across the plains of Africa to shimmering fireflies looking for love . . . I hope you enjoy admiring these animals on the move!

Anna Wright

Sea Turtles

Sea turtles have swum in our warm, tropical seas since dinosaurs roamed the land. They can live to be over a hundred years old, and their bodies and shells are beautifully patterned. When it is time to lay their eggs, the female turtles return to the same nesting point where they were born, sometimes thousands of miles away. Unlike their female partners, male turtles have no reason to return to the land, which means they almost never leave the ocean.

Springboks

South African springboks are very social animals that form huge herds – sometimes tens of millions strong! When disturbed, springboks leap into the air with their legs extended, sometimes as high as four metres! This is called 'pronking'. Springboks are one of the fastest land animals in the world.

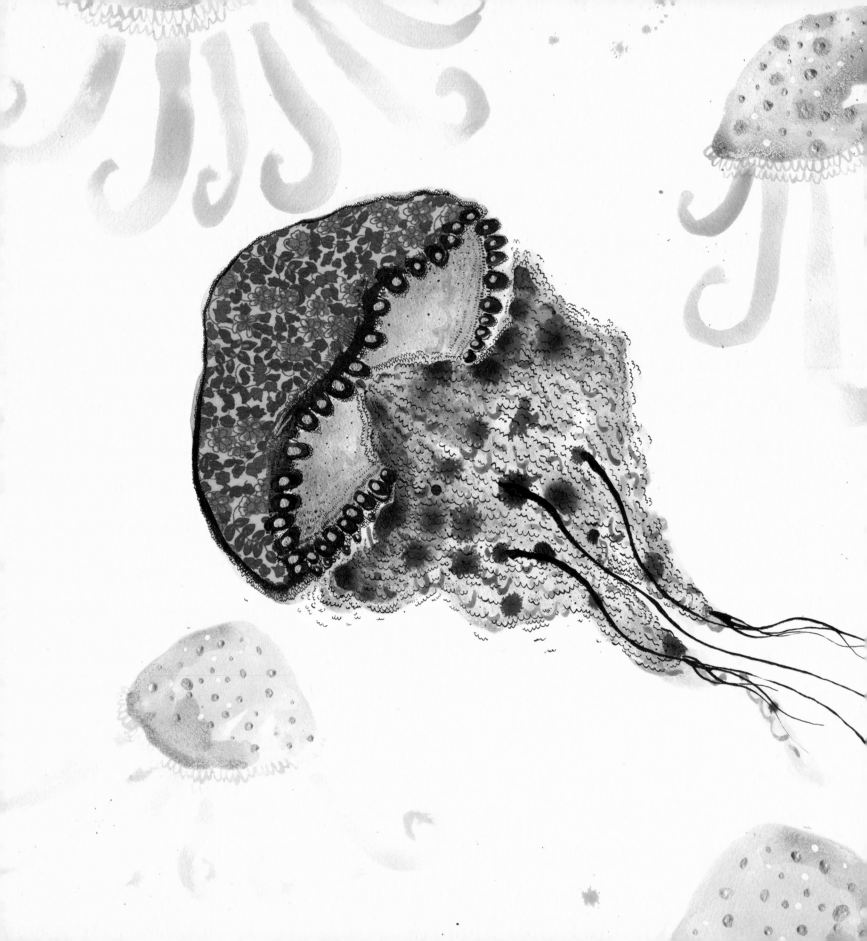

Jellyfish

Jellyfish have been swimming the Earth's oceans for over five hundred million years, and can be found in seas all over the world. These creatures are beautifully translucent and move through the water with incredible grace. When jellyfish swarm it is known as a 'bloom'. If a jellyfish is cut into two, the pieces of jellyfish will survive and create two new jellyfish! Some jellyfish can even glow in the dark.

Crabs

Christmas Island, in the Indian Ocean, is home to millions of large bright-red crabs. Once a year all the crabs migrate from their burrows inland down to the coast. They then mate and their eggs are dropped off into the sea. There are such vast numbers of these migrating crabs that it is hard for motorists to avoid them, so a large bridge and many underpasses have been built for them to cross the roads safely!

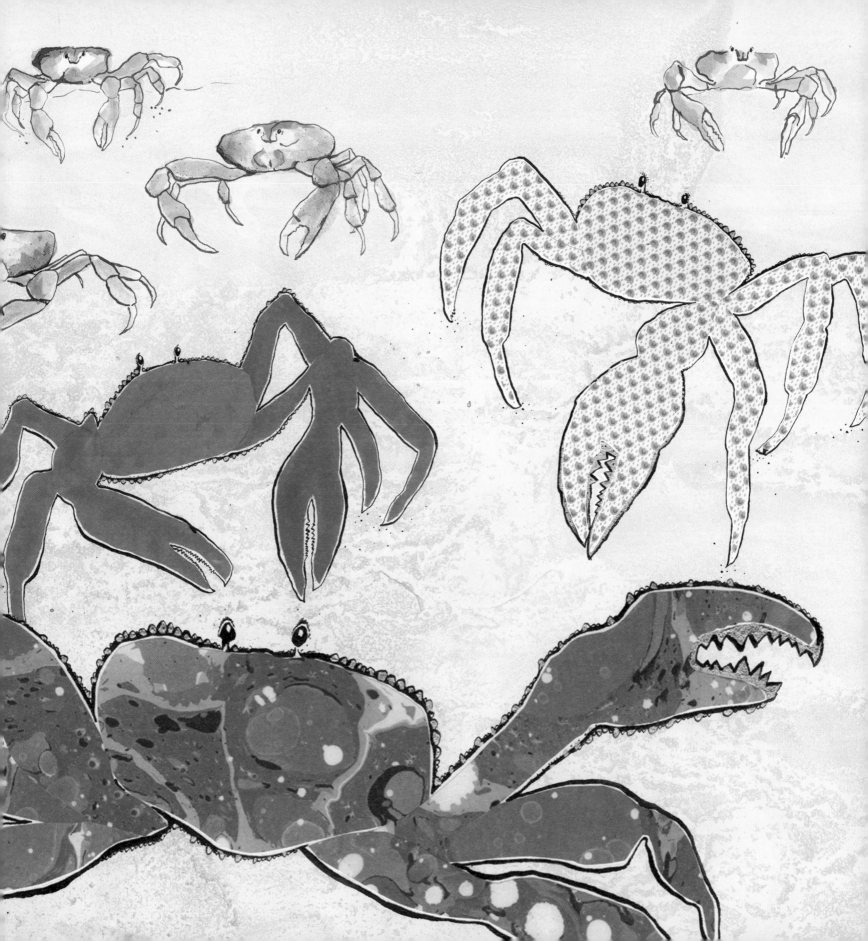

Zebra

Zebra cross the plains of Africa in search of places with plenty to eat, sometimes covering over three hundred miles in one migration. This sight is one of our planet's most awe-inspiring migrations, as well as one of the longest. Each zebra stripe pattern is unique, just like a human fingerprint. When running in a herd, their stripes act as camouflage, making it hard for predators to single out an individual. Clever stripes!

Starlings

During winter, starlings roost together, with some roosting sites hosting over a million birds. From a distance starlings look black, but up close you can see that their feathers are a glossy sheen of purples and greens. Before they settle down for bed, flocks join together in a large swirling mass, creating beautiful swooping patterns in the sky. This incredible sight of thousands of birds moving together is called a 'murmuration'.

Monarch Butterflies

Each autumn, beautifully vivid orange and black monarch butterflies migrate south, from North America to warmer climes in Mexico. They often fly back to the very same tree as their ancestors. The combined weight of so many butterflies can sometimes bend tree branches!

Bumblebees

Bumblebees do not live in hives but in underground burrows. We value them enormously because they help pollinate the plants that we take for granted in our daily lives, such as apples, potatoes and cotton. Bees are excellent pollinators because their coats are so fluffy, they pick up pollen very easily and then transfer it to other plants. Their black and yellow coats also act as a warning to predators – stay away!

Snow Geese

Huge honking flocks of snow geese are a sign of the changing seasons. They fly from North America as far south as Mexico for winter, often travelling in a 'V' formation to minimise the buffeting of the wind. They will honk to encourage those at the front to keep up their speed. They also hold great affection for one another; if one gets sick or wounded a couple of geese may drop out of the 'V' formation to help and protect it. Geese fly back to their northern breeding grounds for the summer. In fact they spend about half the year migrating – to and from the winter and summer resting spots.

Herring

When fish swim tightly together it is called schooling. As one of the most abundant fish species, herring are also the most impressive fish to school, as they collect in such large numbers – up to three billion in one school! They group together like this to defend themselves from predators, as well as enhancing their chances of finding food and a mate. Imagine three billion shimmering silver herring – magnificent!

Southern Carmine Bee-Eaters

Southern carmine bee-eaters nest in burrows dug into the river banks in Africa. As their name suggests, they mainly eat bees – ouch! They are extremely striking in appearance. Deep-red feathers cover most of their bodies, but flashes of bright turquoise adorn their heads and tail feathers. These birds also like to piggyback on to larger animals so that they have a good moving viewpoint from which to target their lunch!

Fireflies

Male fireflies swarm together in their thousands in the hope of wooing a lady firefly. The male uses a mix of air and a special chemical in his body to create a flashing glow. If a female thinks a male has a flashy enough light she will flash back. The fireflies' flickering is their own language of love ...

So when you are next out and about, keep your eyes peeled for magnificent creatures great and small. See if you can spot them wiggle, shimmer or dance. You may be amazed by what you see! We truly do live in a magical world.